ALASTAIR MCINTOSH was raised (
lives with his wife in Greater Gc
Glasgow once famous for buildir
cultural renewal with the GalGael   ...us an honorary
post as Scotland's first Professor of Human Ecology at the
University of Strathclyde.

By the Same Author

Healing Nationhood Curlew Press 2000
Soil and Soul Aurum Press 2001

Love and Revolution

ALASTAIR McINTOSH

Luath Press Limited

EDINBURGH

www.luath.co.uk

First published 2006
Reprinted 2007
Reprinted 2008

ISBN (10): 1-905222-58-0
ISBN (13): 978-1-9-0522258-2

The paper used in this book is recyclable. It is made from
low chlorine pulps produced in a low energy, low emission manner
from renewable forests.

Printed and bound by
Bell & Bain Ltd., Glasgow

Typeset in 11pt Sabon by
3btype.com

For Vérène

Let me say, with the risk of appearing ridiculous, that the true revolutionary is guided by strong feelings of love. It is impossible to think of an authentic revolutionary without this quality.

Che Guevara, *Venceremos*

Contents

Acknowledgements

Most work in this collection is previously unpublished, but some pieces have appeared in prose form in my book, *Soil and Soul* (Aurum Press, 2001).

Homage to Young Men was first performed in January 2006 in King Tut's Wah Wah Hut, Glasgow, with the chart-topping duo Nizlopi (of *JCB Song* fame). This has been released on the band's autumn 2006 album, and I am grateful to the lead singer, Luke Concannon, for permission to reproduce his chorus.

Both *Invocation* and *Homecoming* are drawn from my long poem, *The GalGael Peoples of Scotland*, first published in *Cencrastus* No. 56 (1997). This is available online at www.AlastairMcIntosh.com.

Where well-known literary allusions have been consciously invoked, discreet acknowledgement is usually made through quotation marks.

My warm thanks go out to Tessa Ransford, founder of the Scottish Poetry Library and President of the literary human rights group, Scottish PEN, for her encouragement and advice. Also, to Tess Darwin who first mentored me in the unity of poetics and ecology and who helped with some of the editing. And to Luath Press, especially Gavin MacDougall who has long offered encouragement, and the sharply discriminating eye of Jess Barbier on his editorial staff. I also thank Babs MacGregor, rooted in Lewis, who advised on the cover design, and Rhona MacKinnon, rooted in Harris, for her remarkable cover photography.

Down the years many muses have inspired and mélanged into these poems. Names are not necessary, but I do express my loving gratitude for each fibre of this living filigree.

Introduction

I THINK JOSEPH CAMPBELL was right when he said that all great stories share a common theme. There is the *departure*, when the fresh-faced hero sets out on life's journey; the *initiation*, when she or he hits troubled rapids; and the *return*, bringing back gifts and blessings that help to sustain the community through the process of eldership.

Such is the path of any one of us who rises to vocation's calling. We gradually open out to a life that is greater than our small, egocentric selves. As Campbell concludes: 'The effect of the successful adventure of the hero is the unlocking and release again of the flow of life into the body of the world.'

This calls for nothing less than understanding the real nature of magic. It means seeing our activism, whether it is social or ecological, as spiritual articulation.

Guns are too callous, bombs too ruthless, and knives too blunt to cut the darkness of these times. Our activism demands a poetry that holds out for nothing less than *poesis* – a participation in the beauty of making and re-making reality.

Such calling is to an incarnate politics – to spirituality rendered *carnal*, being engaged with the flesh and fabric that forms our world. That is why love and revolution must be erotically inseparable. That is how we transcend the nihilism of Mark Twain's observation that 'familiarity breeds contempt.' For this spirituality constantly renews the face of the Earth and of weathered humankind.

To work with such forces in a world that is largely oblivious to them inevitably makes one feel, as Ben Okri puts it, that one is transgressing. In writing *Soil and Soul*, I was somewhat able to protect myself behind careful wording and impeccable referencing. But that is less easy to achieve with writing poetry. Here, then, is the underlying naked passion unveiled. It is an offering for all who dare to tread life's elemental ways. Lonely, perhaps, you roam the paths of love, but not alone.

PART I

Departure

Extinction

Have you heard the cry of the curlew?
I tell you –
I would rather we lost
the entire contents
of every art gallery
in the whole world
than lose
forever
the cry of the curlew

The Old Days at Gearranan

The old days interlace with recent memory here
      kelson and ribs round crofting folk's lives
the old days and the lazybeds of the land itself
      bear witness here
sleeping but fecund
      dormant not dead

Crumbling cartwheel arcing out
      half sunk in sheep-shaved field
cracked three-legged blackened pot
      Carron Ironworks Falkirk
whalebones for reminiscence, curiosity
      and maybe luck
black house ruins down every croft
      once ashamed
      but slightly questioning
      now
      tight concrete bungalows
older still, *The Stones*, Calanais
      once dismissed
      but slightly questioning
      now
      religious rectitude

And frugal functionality too:
'Lewis is a place
where else will you see
the head of a bed
where a gate ought to be'

Changing Channels

When TV came in the front door
or so the old folks say
the stories left by out the back
and children ceased to play

but when you look into that fire, says Rusty
the North Lochs blacksmith
intimate since infancy
when you look into Torcuil's fire
into the hearth of the bard of Grimashadar
the heart of the house of the bard of Grimashadar
when you look into that peat fire...
you can see the whole world

see me, says Nicky
the Greater Govan blacksmith
new to my acquaintance
I like to watch the politics of guppies
I've got both a fish tank and a fire
in my wee place
when you're tired of one...
change channels to the other

When TV goes back out the rear
then Govnu's way is taught
from elemental stories forged
an ancient truth is wrought

Climbing Roineabhal

you leave the road
     and scramble over heathery hillocks
        tumbled mossy boulders
           reposed amongst dark bogs

soon you're into little valleys
     with xylophonic streams
        that play a tinkling music
          to their water's fall

rising yet more steeply
     garnets sparkle burgundy in naked rocky clefts
        unveiled by ice-age glaciers
           of last week's virgin birth

pressing on the summit
     Alpines crouch by stone cairn – uttering
        a whistled song – stuttering
          nature's prayer – guttering
            in Himalayan blast

and beyond, the Hebrides
the Holy Hebrides

Origins of a Landscape

they say the hills of the Hebrides
were made by giant women
who lay down long ago
and fell asleep
and turned to stone

beautiful Roineabhal!
all through Kilbride, the threaded Bays of Harris
from fishing boat or winding down the Golden Road
I see your summit's flowing hair swept back

two thousand million years of love
your youthful face stares heavenwards
neck, breasts and belly, legs and even knees
        before the ocean washes feet
                where otters play by Lingerabay

Sithean an Airgid

The *Li* or 'pattern of the Tao'
– a Chinese word derived
from grain of wood or muscle
the just so and the how so
of the suchness of reality

And did you notice me, my love
the way I watched your figured brow
rippling and flickering
feeling and intelligence
a sensitivity as something free and wild
      a deer on Cailleach na Mointeach at Sithean an Airgid
        the Sleeping Beauty Mountain and the
          Silver Faerie Hill
the 'pattern of the Tao,' the *Li*
    of muscle under skin, the *Li*
      of psyche under flesh, the Dharmic *Li*
        of cosmic truth sustaining
          you and me

Murdo of Assynt

I took you to hear the unknown Assynt poet
with tales of tigers crossing by the Forth Road Bridge
and more humanity engrimed upon a finger
than knaves and chancers scrape from all their privilege

And there we found him lying in a doorway
up an alley taking shelter where they go to share a fag
crashed out amongst the boxes and the bottles
huddled embryonic in a frozen sleeping bag

And let us pay respects to Murdo, love
let us eulogise the witness that he rhymes
bard from off the croft cast out on stony ground
canary down the mines of these our troubled times

Eulogy for Finlay Montgomery of North Lochs

The news came in a letter from my father
Aye, the news came across the furthest watery wastes
Attention All Shipping!
in sea area Hebrides…

And all I have now
is the prow of *Hiawatha*
hanging from my wall
by a silver cord
Attention All Shipping!

Crippled Finlay, wise, kindly
of few or no words
who taught small boy to handle
     small boat
          big weather
               Attention! Attention! Attention!

I remember your promise never met, Finlay
to take me fishing
far out there
beyond our normal haunt
the big blue boat
To the Carranoch!
three miles pulling eastwards out from port
an oar's length north of 58th parallel

Broken promise, broken fingernails
Finlay, alone on water
cramped grip on tarry keel
scraped down beneath Loch Grimashadar
goodbye, dear friend

And I shall always slightly fear
the beauty of that sea loch now
the pitiless sea
the shadow side of nature
that we can but accept, accept
and like the next wave, accept

'Very dead,' as you would say
on those rare days we let down baited lines
six fathoms but to no avail

Very dead was how the divers found you
under the whelming tide
beyond the 'furthest Hebrides'
Archangel tar beneath your splintered finger nails
Archangel chorus soaring overhead
Very Dead Dear Finlay
aye, very dead
       in all but memory of your brightness
          setting on the western wave

Attention All Shipping!
    Attention All Shipping!
        Attention All Shipping!
            In Sea Area
            Hebrides! Hebrides! Hebrides!

Attention All Shipping!
    Attention All Shipping!
        Staaaaaaaaand to Attention...
all shipping

God rest his soul
Amen, *agus* Amen

Love in a Killarney Churchyard

it was your voice I heard behind me
your softly yielded breasts that mused me into song
your shimmering touch quickening my limbs
transfiguring carnality
and raising me towards an understanding
perhaps of how another felt when blessed Mary Magdala
poured precious oil upon those feet
and kissed them and kept kissing them
impervious to impropriety
and stroked those feet enfolding them
with tear-soaked loose and tumbling hair
a love surpassing all the world's opprobrium

'But I must be careful with my heart,' you said

'I must be careful of her heart,' I told myself

and now you've gone across the sea
and my heart aches in mortal angst
a deepening Atlantic trough

Journey out of the Hebrides

and you and me, my passing German friend
gazing out from rocky kneecap over surf

nothing but this surging North Atlantic race
holds between us and that other native shore

a rainbow medicine drum beats common time
listen, as our salutations echo on the swell

Boating in Maine

Some things you never lose
like when David took us sailing
sharing thoughts of poetry and form
and rowing back the tender to the pier
I twisted oars in symmetry of perfect counterpoint
an exquisitely executed turn
gliding with precision into dock

He remarked, impressed,
       and I confess a pleasing swell of pride
the thought that skill from Hebridean boyhood held its edge
       thirty years along
            this western bank
                the Great Atlantic

Some things you never lose
like rowing a boat
drift angled, crosswind, no great hurry
we'll arrive, my dear, when time ordains
with strength of arms and keel of oak
as oars dip softly through the diamond sparkle of each wave
and lapping clinker rhythm dapples dancing over larch
and fathomless the melody of currents in my soul
soaring with the poetry of knowing you from inside out
singing to myself from outside in and turned back round again
at being seen by you, desired by you...
...it is your love that I'm in love with...
some things you never lose

Rocky Mountain Walk

The yellowed aspen flutters to the ground
in rocky crag the eagle's wing unfurls
rowan berry splashes mountain red against the sky
spider's web awaits to catch a moment in your eye

You who have no names for all the glories you behold
no science or sharp analysis, nor levers of control
I watch you linger gazing into limpid tumbling pool
loving more than gold the fleeting gravel gathered there

And did you hear, my love, the murmured word last night
of Aborigines who dream the land and walk its way and say
that White Man lies and walks with lies held out before his
    heart
and this is why he talks his walk and talks and talks to such
    excess

But in your skystruck face, I see no lie

Connecticut Woods

framed through this
new england window
spindle birch
maple bow

and i am missing you
softly
incessantly
quivering foliage

Ainm Caraid?

so very sad
to be here
not to know you
not to see
or be seen
inside
by your love
in me
for you

Golgotha Station

Your train gone to meet your flight
        my flight trailing vapour wisps
                of residual imagination
Alone on the platform I weep
        to keep unkeepable loveliness

A white dove lies dead beside a newspaper stand
early morning, undelivered...
...a white dove lies dead, do you hear me?
...dead beside a newspaper stand
Dead or not dead?
Who can tell?
Just shocked, perhaps
by its own so-vulnerable softness
staggered by the *News of the World*
A white dove lies dead, do you hear?
Hypothermia at the very least
frozen through
and frozen out
Shall we warm it?

I'm talking here of loss that feels like death

Unrequited Cosmology

If sun had no moon
    could he still shine?
Is projection really all there was
    to our connection?
Woman as mirror
    man, a terrible burning rite?
Is this the essence of your fear
    that now demands a distance
        that exceeds the speed of light?

PART II

Initiation

The Scyther's Prayer

May my death
be the clean cut
of an honest scythe
and never
the thousand lashes
of an accursed strimmer

Ode to the Upright Uptight of a Scottish Church Society
on Politely Discussing Liberation Theology
at One of the Best Hotels in the Land
and Placing me Effectively
on Trial for
Heresy

If
we are
not very careful
the doors of Heaven
will open wide and we
shall all be engulfed... AND
THERE SHALL BE NO DAMNED

Meeting on the Eve of the First Gulf War

We arrived desolate, frightened, disbelieving, awestruck,
    powerless.
The log fire at Peace House spluttered against a snowy night.
Each one was touched by numbing, prescient shellshock.
A reading from *Reproaches for Good Friday*
    'I brooded over the abyss,
    with my words I called forth creation:
    but you have brooded on destruction,
    and manufactured the means of chaos....'
Long silences.
Coloured flumes from spurting logs.
Beautiful. Cosy. But too hot inside.
Too hot for children's touch.
Too hot to spray on humankind.
Even on soldiers, damn them (damn us!)
Someone's son or someone's daughter.
Someone's husband, mother, lover.
These targets are too REAL to burn.

War in the Gulf: Not in My Name
    say the button badges.
And the agenda – listening time on the agenda.
Each speaks to their condition.
Silence. Tears. Holding.
Powerless?
    perhaps.
Disempowered?
    never.

After Culloden

The Highland Clearances
hard recruiting sergeants
Scottish regiments for English battles
potato famine
later economic dearth
and half a million Scots
    not to mention Irish
        directly or by circumstance
            driven from their land

As was for the Iraqi Kurds
        so was for the Gaelic ones
'You see,' said the Iranian scholar:
        'We are looking at a common history'
an archetypal commonality
of suppurating colonisation
perpetuation and re-perpetuation
    broken emigrants breaking First Nations
        hunting Aborigines, indenturing Africans
            Calvinist Apartheid
                oppressed turned oppressor
                    lowest common denominator of brutality

And England!
You carver-up of nations for perpetual advantage!
Divided self's divide-and-rule worldview
Yes, you, England!
dear England

you too were cleft within your soul
viscerally cauterised
    much further back in time
        by Roman and by Norman yokes
           of robber barons
                lords of war and land
                    that laid you low

But still I sense your taproot yet
to winnow from the karmic curse
Winstanley's England, Blake and Mary Webb
Benjamin Zephaniah and Elizabeth Fry
and George Monbiot in the Manchester *Guardian*
and even a Great Chain
        of Liverpool Bishops
           grooving with Jah people
                in their struggle, their desperation
                    their elation and their elevation

And did those feet on green and pleasant land?
Of course they did!
Aye... England...
Sill writhing in the birth pangs of your great vocation
See you, England...
Jerusalem England!

Walking Barefoot in a 3-Piece Suit in Glasgow

*In protest at the plight of fleeing Kurds
barefoot and starving after the First Gulf War*

at first i feared
i'd be ashamed
but now i'm proud
and I recall
how crossing through
Saint Enoch's Square
I trod each step
in dignity

Transfiguration

barefoot, you know the touch of flesh on earth
some rivulets are warming to the step
they've long flowed over sunny slopes
and others keekit coyly from the spring
...they're the icy-feeling ones
to cup the hands and drink

and you tread the ground more gently
      when out walking in this way
you don't cut in with hard-heeled boots
      but softly contour toes
          to grip the land on equal footing
leaning forwards better seeing what is waiting to be found there
on passing by unharming over emerald sod set in
with mandalas of *tormentil* that salve the heart pursed open now
a golden blossomed harmony, a sermon of small things

Invocation

Ohhh... friends we call across the seas to you from echo
    chamber of the soul
We call now stirred by rhythm that you drum
We call upon the triple billion year old songlines of world's
    oldest rock
'I lift a stone; it is the meaning of life I clasp' – says the bard
    MacDiarmid
So let us honour stone. Let us call afresh the foundational
    litany:
The Lewisian Gneiss...
The Cairngorm pegmatites and sparkling Aberdeenshire granite
The Old Red Sandstone
The Durness limestone sequences and Bathgate's forest
    Carboniferous
The Tertiary radiating basalt dykes from great volcanoes Mull
    and Raasay
The Sgurr of Eigg and Ailsa Craig
The idle pebbles...
tossed to and fro, round and round, inwards outwards
dark moon full moon vortexing on today's high tide at noon
Ohhh... the rocks the rocks the rocks
we call on you ...
Rise up from sleep sunk strata beds!
Giant women, wizened men, totemic creatures once laid down
    to be our hills
Wake up! Wake up! Wake up and waulk this Earth in us!
...bring back the land within the people's care
...bring back the care to touch from hand to land

Epistle to the Laird of Eigg

On becoming the first man to sell and buy his own island

Wealth,

> may have won you back
> the legal title to a little Scottish island
> control of livelihoods and homesteads
> but you can never own
> an island's soul
> or that of those
> whose lives
> here paint their meaning

Soul,

> naught less
> is what's in question
> your claim to right of title
> hath no moral weight
> it is but overcompensation
> for the grandiose vacuity
> of the idolatrous faith
> that to *have* means to *Be*

Land,
>   remember
>   is the bedrock from which we find
>   sustenance and grounding
>   to glorify and enjoy
>   (at last, long last, enjoy!)
>   the wellspring of Creation
>   forever
>   and ever

Desist,
>   from fancied ownership
>   make this bad title good
>   and may you be so honoured
>   and may your heart be warmed
>   in justified assurance
>   as you walk with us a friend
>   amongst community
>   of place

Tom Forsyth of the Isle of Eigg Trust

Tom Forsyth of Scoraig
Trustee in Waiting.
Trustee in what?
Of Eigg, that 'favoured isle'?
Oh yes – but not just waiting.
Trustee. That says it all.
Aye – Tom Forsyth, crofter.
Guardian of land usufruct
     and spoiler of free market spoils.
Trustee of Iona
     and friend of George and Borstal boys.
Trustee of Eigg
     and knower of the little white rose
          that smells so sharp and sweet
               'and breaks the heart.'
Professor of Maieutic Vocation
     specialised in
          ancient philosophy, crofting and
               the mid-life crisis.
Trustee. Trusting. Trusted. Truth.
Quaker of the heart
     and to hell with set formalities.
Arsonist of burnt-out form
     to hell, transfiguring even Hell.
'Out on a limb,' you'd say
     'for that is where the blossom grows.'
Sailing in your boat
     where ere the wind of spirit blows.
A witness to God's providence
     the beauty that your knowledge shows...
Prophet, indeed, *Trustee*.

The Forge

What is the point of land reform
so that remote communities
can be preserved
as threatened cultures
at a massive social cost
to the nation as a whole
of teachers, doctors, police and ferry services
when most of those raised native from such soil
are now so few and only have two kids
who've mostly moved elsewhere to stay
their burns and braes seductive now
to ever-higher bidders from away
with little thought or want for joining in
God's rhythm of the crofters' passing day...
and most who 'ever mattered' here
are dead or spread or going gone
the beauty of a people's life
strewn like cemetery flowers
and even markings on the land
are fossils fading down the years
with only gales and rain to carve
a soaring waterfall, of tears?

Either we turn our faces to the wall
burn out, sell out
or jumping from the bridge
choose at least the honest statement of
heartbreak hotel's check-out...
or else we muscle down
      roll up our sleeves
           and dig from where we stand
to shovel ruddied muddied ores of melded human sand
and stoke the glowing hearth anew to smelt and skim and
    pour
a precious shimmering stream refined by sense of place and
    ancient lore
(like hodden lead ripped off in time from round the ruin's sill
and fired until it crumbles to a freshened mercurial rill)
then on the ringing anvil to a meteor shower of sparks
we strike the tempering ingot, dreaming new and old hallmarks
... *and hammer out the beauty, of the braided crofting way...*
which is our greatest export, to this world that's gone astray...
and *that's* the point of land reform
      in the politics
        of today.

MacMugabe?

This clearance of white landowners on Lewis
thunderethed the *Telegraph*
is but the Mugabification
of the Hebrides

See you...
I told my African friend
doe-eyed musician and a man of peace
raging passion for land reform
and yet himself a refugee
from calloused old Mugabe

See you...
I implored him
I look to the day with Livingstone
when Scotland will become
an honorary member
of the Organisation
for African Unity

Meanwhile, brother
for a' that and a' that
you're here for quality control

Saddhu Livingstone

You're not in good shape
I told my friend straight
your dog's gone your luck's down
your body's lost weight

and you live in a van your home
burnt to the groun'
by arsonist vandals
adrift from the town

See me, Livvy said
in the old Brechin Bar
that's just mah whole life
it's the fate of mah star

for the more they come on me
and more that all's gone
the more that all's left
is mah spiritual song

Benediction for Cathy Collard on her Deathbed

I do not know about cures
but the end of healing
is to reconcile this crucifixion
with all time's
this death
with life eternal

we must push deeper
underground
into the awaiting Hill

the healing of the faeries be with you, Cathy
the healing of the angels be with you, Cathy
the healing of Christ Almighty, with you, Cathy

God rest her soul
Amen, *agus* amen

Inner Decolonisation

The weight of air was stiff
this thick December day
with fish and chip shop soggy frying
acrid bus brakes sharply crying
an old demoniac slowly dying
broken hopes and dribbled sighing
inner chains of Prozac buying...
a Roman peace at Govan Cross
that Pictish kings called, desolation

But my mind somehow shifts on high
transfigured to an island sky
the air now thick with fish boats docking
the screech of brakes, just seagulls flocking
the power of love engaged in breaking
Legion's mad imperial raping
inner crusts of bondage flaking...
the Peace of God at Gadarene Cross
that Christ called, liberation

PART III

Return

Beatitude

Blessed are the passionate
      for they shall be lovemakers in eternity

Scotland

A person belongs
inasmuch as they are willing
to cherish and be cherished
by this place
and its peoples

Homage to Young Men

Chorus by Nizlopi's Luke Concannon

I want to talk to all the young men out there
It's for the women too, but especially the men,
    'cos it's tough to be a young man in this world
You have to face so much heartbreak and loss
In love and career and life
It's easy to forget the meaning and give up
To burn up or sell out to addictions, despair or greed
Easy to forget that life's a journey
    with a beginning, a middle and an end
It's about navigating the future, your future
It's about learning to become a man who's real,
    and able to love

    Are you waiting for me?
    Are your hands down in the dirt?
    We belong together
    I've been longing since my birth
    To be arms around you
    To be true to who we are
    To let all our pain out
    To be playing in your heart

So let's talk about the first stage of life
The departure, when your boat is pushed out on the river
Most of who you are is still your small self
The you your family has made you,
    your schooling and your friends

You've still not found your deep self, your Great Self,
      'cos that's what the journey's for
So you set out, full of hope, but with a heavy load
All the baggage of your upbringing
All the love, yes, but the fucked-up-ness too
Maybe the absent father, or the smothering mother,
      or the cold indifference of those around you
It's no wonder you've a rough ride coming
It's gonna get tough and it's got to
So you can find your Self
So you can become, a real man

And that's when you hit the second stage of life
The initiation in the rapids and the storms
That's when you find the pain of brokenheartedness
Love affairs that fail, failures in career
      and all your hopes for what the world might have been
Plenty young men founder grazed on such jagged rocks as these
Bruised and angry in a storm of violence towards self and others
But it doesn't have to stay like that
No, my friends, not if you push on and open to the inner grace
      that will bring you courage
The courage to face reality as it is,
      without lies
The courage to know your wound but to outgrow it
      and insist on beauty
The courage to open your heart,
      to hold fast to truth,
          and to stand each step in dignity

And that's the courage that brings your boat to the third stage
    of life
To see how your small self is held in a greater Self
And that you're fit to be an elder in your community,
    able to share the gifts and the blessings
Able to support and inspire what gives life among your people
And to love your beloved,
    to love and be loved by *the Beloved* no less, my friends
Because we're talking here of love in all its meanings
And you can only love with a deepening heart
And that is why you had to grow courage on this journey to
    the ocean
That's what your battle wounds on the field of life were all
    about
That, my dear friends,
      is what qualifies you
            to be a man in your community
Capable of loving and able to be loved...
Capable of loving
    and able to be loved...
Capable of loving
    and able
        to be
            loved

The Geometry of Infinity

By definition, the mathematicians say,
parallel lines 'meet at infinity'
Anything less they'd cross
and not remain in parallel
And infinity never comes
except in eternity
And so, in this world
the lines remain parallel
always equidistant
yet inching
to an infinite
reconciliation

I've been thinking so it is with us
In loving you I yearn to find a union
one God-nature drawn from out us both
And yet there's always the lacuna
loss or reservation plus the fear of death
and also sacred space wherein the soul unfolds
that Merton called
'the sanctuary
      of another's
           subjectivity'

I used to worry about this gap
Would love somehow be always unrequited?
And then I thought of parallel lines
meeting at infinity
uniting in eternity
and I turned on the radio
and the songs were all about you
loving you beyond this life
outside confines of time and space
dying to and dying for
and dying in 'forever and a day'
like Sufi hymns
the Song of Songs
Saint John of the Cross
on *Top of the Pops*
...and they call it Radio Ga Ga?
...Radio Jah Jah, I'd say!

Blessing

In the Februaries of your life
may you find warmth
by blazing hearths
of honest kindness
congregated choirs
of sparkling logs
that kindle one another
to community

and may the sap
of all you yearn
be limpid pressed
with peaty nose
and flowing poured
to raise a glass
that sparkles rainbows
round your eyes

On the Beach

And I moved with you
      into a cave beneath the sea
As we made love
      to the rhythm of our soul
          the tide of being
You laughed
      as my beard was the tangle
And I saw starfish
      in your eyes
         taking me cosmic
            big dipper rides
               on the surf of time

Moontime

I watched a stalwart
candle in the dark
scintillate diamonds
on this ocean-tumbled rock

Quartz turning hornblende
waxen and waned
shimmering facets
throne for a queen

And you reposed there
so ruby and mellow
moistening moontime
claret and honey

As you asked...
with such
unnecessary consideration...
if I minded the time

Wife

kissing you
     is like kissing
         a bed of flowers
but this is what every bed of flowers
     has ever aspired
        to be

Pearly Gates

morning glory
wild abandon
richly intertwined

warm dark soil
and brightening skies
both our souls combined

At the Dark Moon

It was with John Seed on the Nightcap trail
ten days we activists had walked
Mount Nardi and Protestors' Falls
and now as evening stillness fell
starlight waxed on dark moon night
yes, stillness fell as Alison
began to call Her names

Isis... Astarte... Diana...
      Hecate... Demeter... Kali...
        ...Innana

Like a train in the night so soft at first
She came a quickening presence
low murmuring with the trees and flames
it swelled, our song, we rose and danced
a-whirling waist-bare round the fire
in utter orgiastic wildness

So it was She came to us
black-skinned the darkness
      fecund
         jewelled
with stars that overflowed
      this Net of Indra's Milky Way
         revealed from Goddess breasts
            unveiled to us by cosmic
              dark moon sky

Lithogenesis of the Feminine

'All is lithogenesis' – *MacDiarmid*

She needs the space to form herself
release gas bubbles from that molten lens
plutonic settling into how She comes to pass
traversing eons of Tardis time
and slowly cooling
stratifying
differentiation and
distinction uttered incarnate
and wondrous is this process to behold
and crystal is this tender gem

And did you know
that crystal structure
plucks its strength
not from pristine spotlessness
but from minute impurities
that interlock the lattice layers
amongst the sparkling molecules
an elemental fortitude
out of adoption born?

Ah! the ingenuity of being igneous
this sister, mother, lover of the world
no wonder wise men whisper
in Her footsteps
'holy – holy – holy'
knowing that
there is no god but God

Epiphany

I love the way you gather us beneath your wing of prayer
I love the lightness rightness even the right-on-ness
the way you pray the way that lovers do it
spume of fiery lava melding merging
spiritual tectonics... and do you know that
I-just-tripped-out-on-your-eyes...
the kindness lines
that radiate around your eyes
the light of God almighty
shining in Your eyes

Tree of Life

We parted by the garden gate
       when love's new world was bright
Our souls were made of stardust, dear
       but feet were clad in night
And often when we'd pause for breath
       we'd feel the throbbing pain
And yearn for one another's smile
       and kisses soft as rain

As mountains rose and cities fell
       and ice floes reached the sea
I sifted through the ravished wastes
       and you in turn sought me
We faced the pipes of hardship, love
       transcending drums of pride
Polished by vicissitude
       like pebbles on the tide

Confronting brute realities
       but helming by the sky
Sailing through eternity
       from death to life to die
Mellow is the colour, dear
       of my soul's love for you
And apples are the taste by which
       you'll know my love is true

And mellow is the colour, dear
  of my soul's love for you
And apples are the taste by which
  you know my love is true
We parted by the garden gate
  when God's new world was bright
Our hearts are now enfolded, love
  in Tree of Life's birthright

Good News from a Rough Year

And we laugh!
such fulsome laughter!
we catch each other's eyes
and know
and overflow
and this love is the life that matters
this ecology of requiting relationship
this acceptance of surface reality
and its holding in the deep beyond...
here is our dance
and our awakening is
      the small dream opening
          to the great
as flowing out
we wink back to the stars
our sanity affirmed
our hearts confirmed
'stardust... and golden'
some good things
      have happened
         this past year
and all shall be well
'and all manner of thing'
shall be so very well

Homecoming

Dear fellow creatures
native brothers sisters children
in other heartlands of the real, the reel
We ask from you acceptance
of our peoplehood
We ask you weave our native threads
to fabric of one scintillating cloth
that is the mantle of the world
We pledge to you support
for all work sourced in love
recovering right relationship your territories
And ask from you forgiveness
for past injustice, ignorance and spoils of fear or greed
We need your help with Spirit's grace
to find clear paths through tangled modern *Waste Land* tares
to seed as oaks as gods each one proclaiming Jubilee
To fly in fair formation as wild geese...
To hear afresh that deep poetic story
of magic set in time when place began...
To make a life worth living...
To save this Earth...
...And play from down the hollow hill
A hallowed music
Sacred dance
That is our soul...
...our soil

Notes to Some of the Poems

Climbing Roineabhal and *Origins of a Landscape*: Roineabhal (*Roin-è-val*) mountain in the National Scenic Area of Harris was threatened with being turned into the biggest roadstone quarry in the world by the English company, Redland. Redland then got taken over by Lafarge from France, and in 2005 executives from Paris formally withdrew from the project in a splendid Auld Alliance gesture of 'corporate social responsibility,' after what had been a thirteen-year-long battle. Thus Roineabhal's status as a 'sacred mountain' was confirmed.

Meeting on the Eve of the First Gulf War: The poem describes the meeting of Scottish Churches Action for World Development at Peace House on the eve of the first Gulf War, at which we decided to circumvent the government's declared preparedness to censor news (including peace movement activities) by setting up *GulfWatch*. This was a daily news digest sent primarily to Scottish church leaders, and subsequently, as we discovered, reprinted and circulated all over the world, including the United States, New Zealand and Pakistan. What was distinctive at the time was that we had access (through 'GreenNet') to what is now called the internet, but which in 1991 was almost unknown. This meant we were able rapidly to pull in news from both international and insider sources. To the best of our knowledge, it was the first time that the internet had been used, certainly in Britain, overtly to circumvent state censorship. An extensive digest was published as Issue 89 of the *Edinburgh Review* in 1993. It remains available as a resource on my website (Google 'mcintosh gulf-watch'). *Reproaches for Good Friday* was written by the liturgist Janet Morley.

Walking Barefoot in a 3-Piece Suit in Glasgow: This poem derives from the immediate aftermath of co-editing *GulfWatch* with my colleague, Alastair Hulbert. As Kurdish refugees fled, barefoot and starving, over the mountain passes in the winter of early 1992, we in the peace movement felt outraged that the British state, that had done so much to fight this war, did so little to address the suffering it had set loose after years of propping up and arming a tyrant like Saddam Hussein. At that time it felt as if mainstream Britain had resumed normality by turning its face away from outrage. In witness to this, I donned a three-piece suit, and for three days went about my normal work – at the Centre for Human Ecology then in Edinburgh University, at a board meeting of the Scottish Catholic International Aid Fund in Glasgow, etc. – walking completely barefoot and carrying a placard that read: 'The Kurds – barefoot, starving'. It was one of those moments of profound activist discomfort – not so much because there was ice on the pavements (I was amazed at how the feet stayed warm provided the body was warm), but rather, because of the acute embarrassment. It was just something that I had to do because of what was being done in our names, though my self-consciousness was such that I avoided press publicity. Little wonder that, around this time, I started to take some comfort from the Old Testament prophets, since what I was up to wasn't as bad as Isaiah at least. According to chapter 20:3 of his Biblical biography, he 'walked naked and barefoot for three years... as a sign and a portent'. Ouch! After just three days footloose, it seems I got off lightly!

Invocation and *Homecoming*: Both of these are taken from my long poem, *The GalGael Peoples of Scotland*. This was written at the Pollock Free State motorway protest in Glasgow, at the request of a convention of Native Americans who had asked us to state our vision for contemporary indigenous identity. In Scottish Gaelic, the *Gall* are the strangers (as in such place names as Galloway and Galway), and the *Gael* are the heartland people. The term 'Gall-Gael' people originated in 9th century Scotland, when there had been such a lot of interbreeding with the Norse in parts of the western seaboard that Gaels in this area became so named to suggest that they were 'strange' or 'foreign'. This offers a powerful metaphor for how most of us are today. There's a mélange of both the Gall and the Gael in nearly everybody, thus the expression used in the full version of the poem, 'We're all GalGael now.' It is from this potentially inclusive sense of identity that we must carve a new sense of *being* community of place in order to *care* for community of place between both people and nature. The full poem of *The GalGael Peoples of Scotland*, with its extensive footnotes, was first published in *Cencrastus* (Issue 56, 1997) and is available online at www.AlastairMcIntosh.com. It was mainly to live closer to the GalGael Trust (founded by the late Colin Murdo Macleod) that my wife, Vérène Nicolas, and I moved to Govan in 2004. For more information see also www.GalGael.org.

Epistle to the Laird of Eigg: The Isle of Eigg Trust was set up in 1991 by Tom Forsyth, Bob Harris, Liz Lyon and myself, to challenge landed power in a modern context. The catalyst on Eigg was a Court of Session ruling that ordered the laird, Keith Schellenberg, to sell the island to terminate what had been an ongoing business arrangement with his former wife, the Honourable Margaret de Hauteville Udny-Hamilton. This epistle was written originally in prose form and published in *Reforesting Scotland* (Issue 7) in 1992 after he duly complied with the ruling, but then bought Eigg back through his own holding company! Temporarily, he thereby thwarted the land reform effort. The wonderful line about never being able to buy an island's soul was given to me, and quoted as being from me, by a journalist on the *West Highland Free Press* at the time.

Tom Forsyth of the Isle of Eigg Trust: The Isle of Eigg Trust's response to the Laird of Eigg buying back his own island was to re-affirm that we comprised a Damoclean 'Trust in Waiting'. The Sword of Damocles was suspended from a single horsehair above a fool who wanted to play at being the king, symbolising that the fool's power is always transient. Later on, as the reality of community land ownership materialised on Eigg in 1997, I came to see the Laird as having been a Wizard of Oz-like figure. He had unwittingly, but wonderfully, drawn from all who walked his Yellow Brick Road the magic of courage, empathy and acumen. So, a big 'thank you' to *Laird Emeritus* Keith Schellenberg! Tom Forsyth was in many ways my mentor and a kind of muse throughout this journey. He is particularly fond of Hugh MacDiarmid's poem, *The Little White Rose* – the Scots or Burnett rose – which grows wild in profusion on Eigg and which, for both Forsyth and MacDiarmid, had totemic significance.

The Forge: It is worth sharing a peculiar happening during the writing of *The Forge*, a piece that draws out the GalGael principles of re-made indigenous identity as described in the notes to *Invocation* and *Homecoming* above. The poem took form during a Strathclyde University Human Ecology student field trip to the Isle of Eigg in April 2006. I woke up with some images strong in my mind, and worked them into a draft before breakfast. The previous night we'd viewed *Hallaig* – Timothy Neat's moving documentary about the Skye bard, Sorley MacLean – and had discussed why there are so few indigenous people now remaining on places like Eigg. We were saddened at the decline of such an elementally and relationally rich way of life and the superficial and even 'virtual' reality of so much that replaces it.

As I penned the piece, I was approached by Ewen Hardie, a Scottish student who, like myself, had worked as a ghillie and stalker's pony boy with the wise MacRae family of keepers on the Eisken Estate of Lewis. Not having any idea what I was writing, Ewen told me that he'd like to share a dream from the previous night. He had found himself in the company of a design student who was working on a 'T-shirt for the future.' He travelled forward in time with her and they arrived at the door of a flat. Here were two young men. Both were nervous, but the designer took them outside to 'try out' her T-shirt. The scene then shifted to a weathered old woman working at a forge in an industrial landscape. She was now the one wearing the T-shirt, and it proved to have remarkable properties. Every time she hammered the hot metal on her anvil the landscape changed. From one of constructed forms lit by a sharply flashing electric light, it became a place of rolling hills bathed in sunlight, filled with birdsong and other happy sounds ringing from the anvil. I then read Ewen my draft of *The Forge*. He was astonished at such coincidence. It opened up discussion amongst us of the importance of shared visionary and symbolic experience in discerning the evolution of community. We also reflected that in Scottish Celtic tradition, blacksmithing is considered a magic art under the patronage of Bhrighde of the Hebrides, St Bride. To me, she was the woman in Ewen's dream – the triune maiden (student), mother (with the men) and elemental crone. Again, the archetypal patterning of departure, initiation and return.

My reference to everyone who 'ever mattered' is from Hugh Maclennan, a leading exponent of (European) Canadian national identity, who in a much-quoted passage wrote:

> Such sweeps of emptiness I never saw in Canada before I went to the Mackenzie River. But this Highland emptiness, only a few hundred miles above the massed population of England, is a far different thing from the emptiness of our own North West Territories. Above the 60th parallel in Canada you feel like nobody but God had ever been there before you, but in these deserted Highland spaces around Kintail you feel that everyone who ever mattered is dead and gone.

Lithogenesis of the Feminine: I was a student at Aberdeen in the 1970s and took the 'natural philosophy' classes (that's what 'physics' was properly then called in great Scottish universities) of the famous Professor R.V. Jones. The crystallographic insights expressed here are straight from 'Reggie's' lectures. He was an original English eccentric, with wonderful stories about tricking the Germans with practical jokes during the development of radar in the Second World War. Indeed, the CIA created an R.V. Jones Intelligence Award in 1993 to honour those whose accomplishments mimicked his style, namely, 'Scientific acumen applied with art in the cause of freedom'. Reggie's lectures were never to be missed, though their arguable apogee in this poem would doubtless have left the practical joker scratching his head and wondering if I had been the departmental mis-select that I undoubtedly was.

I would like to say something here that applies to *Lithogenesis of the Feminine* and to several other poems such as *At the Dark Moon* and *Tree of Life*. My work is sometimes too Christian for the 'pagans', and too 'pagan' for the Christians. It's tempting just to say 'too bad', but to do so would disrespect devout persons on both sides of what I see as ultimately being a false dichotomy. Just as non-Christians will ask me, 'Why do you bother with all that baggage – you'd be much more free and accessible without it?' so Christians sometimes puzzle over points of rectitude. This issue does matter to me because I come from a Hebridean community. I find much of the organised religion of our islands problematic, but their applied spirituality has been deeply inspirational. Living today in One World I therefore want to bridge worlds, convinced that the Holy Spirit cannot have been active only for the past two thousand years and in the cultures of the Middle East and the West. I believe this calls us to relationship not only with other faiths that are grounded in love, but also to the inclusive gendering of the divine.

It always puzzles me how conventional non-Christian feminists and conventional patriarchal Christians alike consider such terms as 'God,' 'Christ,' and 'Goddess' to be incompatible with one another. To such feminists, I would urge reflection on what it means for women to give birth to men, and how Mary so splendidly trumped the patriarchy of her time by participating in the upping of the ante of her pregnancy to nothing less than divine status. And to Christians of patrifocal inclination, I would urge consideration of the following Biblical references to the masculine/feminine wholeness of God: a) the likeness of God being both female and male in Genesis 1:27; b) God's 'womb' twice being mentioned as the source of Creation in Job 38; c) the spiritually erotic metaphor of the *Song of Solomon*; d) God's 'woman wisdom' or *Sophia* 'darling and delight' in Proverbs 8; e) Jesus' self-identification as woman wisdom's spokesman in Matthew 11; and, f) even Paul's reminder in Galatians 3 that 'Christ' is beyond such categories as male and female. Such 'scripture proofs' beg consideration that to see God as being exclusively male or female is misguided, even heretical, and that within the constraints of human language it ought be as meaningful to refer to She as He.

My emphasis on the feminine in some of these poems therefore aims to correct a balance that has too often been lost. As for the spirit-filled *carnality* of some of my work, are we not talking in the Christian tradition, though not exclusively to that, of a theology that is very flesh and blood – indeed, *incarnate*? And are we not talking about human love ultimately being embedded in, and drawing us towards, nothing less than eternal divine love – heavenly community as the 'communion of the saints' where we 'become participants of the divine nature' (2 Peter 1:4) because we 'are gods' (Psalms 82:6; John 10:34)? Are we not speaking, then, of possible human relationships that are sacred or mystical, like we find so beautifully expressed in the traditional Anglican marriage service of the *Book of Common Prayer* which includes the pledge, 'With my Body I thee *worship*'? (Worship not *as God*, but most certainly, *in God*.) And are there not parallels in other faiths, like in the Tantric union of 'Sky Dancer' Yeshe Tsogyel with Padma Sambhava, the man credited with bringing Buddhism from India to Tibet?

Such are some implications of the mystical experience that all life is profoundly interconnected in God as love. Our part in that, if we choose to be chosen by it, is what Jesus in John 15 describes as branches on the Vine of Life – because we're all 'members one of another' (Romans 12:5). All religions that are grounded in love come to the same conclusion. Christians call it the Church, Moslems the *Ummah* and Buddhists the noble *Sangha*. That's what love leads to; it has to be, because that individuality in commonality is what love *is*. That's what defines spirituality as being about that which gives life; specifically, life as love made manifest. Such cosmic mystical union is the underpinning of all true community. It is 'human ecology' as the totality of our relationship with elemental nature, human nature and God's nature.

The last line in this poem embraces the central Islamic confession of faith: 'There is no god but Allah.' What a wonderful antidote to all idolatries, including religious gender hegemony! As Moslem feminist theologians are showing, Mohammed (peace be upon him) was a feminist relative to the suffocatingly patriarchal culture of his time. And why should a male prophet, or even a male poet, be so concerned about feminism? Because it's all about *love and revolution* – that's why!

Glossary

POETRY IS A PAIN when terms unfamiliar to the reader are used. I find in my work that people's lives and backgrounds vary so greatly that even shared understanding of words like 'community' can no longer be taken for granted. Here are some of my own, perhaps idiosyncratic, definitions of words used in this book.

Ainm Caraid	'Soul friend' in Celtic spiritual traditions – there are several spelling variations.
Amen *agus* amen	Amen, and again, amen – the customary Gaelic ending to prayer.
Archangel Tar	Thick, black pine tar with a richly evocative smell used to make boats watertight, named after Archangelsk in northern Russia; also called 'Stockholm tar'.
Bard	A shamanic poet who speaks to the psycho-spiritual condition of the people.
Beloved, the	God as lover.
Bhrighde	Bridgit or Saint Bride, the Celtic mother goddess and Christian saint, associated with fire, poetry, craftwork (especially blacksmithing) and the oystercatcher bird.
Brae	Scots (from Old Norse) for a hillside or slope, especially with a path or road running down.
Burn	Scots for a small river (from an Indo-European root-word).

Canary	On account of their acute sensitivity canaries were taken down into coalmines to warn of danger. If the canary passed out, it meant that noxious gases were present and the miners should evacuate.
Community	Interdependence and even interconnection – membership one of another.
Croft	A place on the land that can be lived with, if not from. Crofting as we know it today was first formally established with the 1886 Crofting Act, granting heritable secure tenure.
Crofting	Subsistence livelihood in a crofting community, usually based on seeking providential sufficiency from diverse activities rather than profligate surplus from intensive specialisation.
Culloden	The last battle on mainland British soil, 16 April 1746, at which predominantly Scottish Highland forces were brutally defeated near Inverness.
Dharma	*Dharma* (Sanskrit) or *dhamma* (Pali) is reality understood as the unfolding of natural law, but 'law' is, in my view, too rigid and western a concept properly to capture what, in Quaker parlance, we would call the 'opening of the way.' See also *karma*.
Ego	The 'outer' part of ourselves that comprises the conscious 'I'.

Epiphany	A sudden manifestation of meaning or essence, especially God.
Fathom	A beautifully human nautical measure of just under two metres – the approximate distance of two arms outstretched, as when measuring lengths of rope. Its application in 'sounding' the depth of oceans provides the expression 'unfathomable' for matters deeper than we can ever get to the bottom of.
Filigree	Delicate, intricate, ornamentation from twisted silver or gold wire, or like criss-crossed twigs in woods against a winter sky.
Gaderene	The place where Jesus met the self-harming demoniac who was possessed by Legion, the spirit of Roman colonialism (Mark 5).
Golden Road	The old road winding down the south-east coast of Harris, thought by many to be so named for its great beauty, but actually on account of the cost of building it.
Golgotha	The hill outside Jerusalem where Jesus was crucified – 'the place of the skull'.
Govan	The former shipbuilding area of Glasgow – one of the most socially deprived parts of Western Europe, derived from the Gaelic word for 'smith' (see Govnu).
Govnu	The Celtic blacksmith god, (under patronage of Bhrighde), after whom Govan is named.

Hebrides	The Atlantic string of Scottish islands, north of Ireland, west of the British mainland. The name probably derives from their ancient designation, *Innis Bhrighde* – the Isles of Bridgit.
Hodden	A coarse cloth formerly worn by the peasantry of Scotland, characterised by its grey appearance, which was achieved by mixing black and white wool.
Igneous	Rocks originating from molten magma coming from beneath the Earth's surface crust. These are 'extrusive' when poured out onto the surface (for example, lavas), and 'intrusive' when crystallised deep underground (for example, granite).
Incarnation	Spirit interpenetrating flesh, especially divine indwelling in Jesus.
Isis, etc.	Isis, Astarte, Diana, Hecate, Demeter, Kali and Innana – all names for God as Goddess in ancient cultures.
Jah	Rastafarian word for God.
Jubilee	The Biblical principle of wealth, including land, being periodically redistributed on cycles of seven or fifty years.
Karma	The Sanskrit root of the verb, 'to do,' applied to the law of cause and effect and the way in which prior actions shape future reality. Thus in one of John Seed's songs,

'karma is the things you do; dharma is what comes to you.'

Keekit	Peeped (Scots).
Kelson	The inner keel of a boat to which the ribs are attached – its spinal column. 'And that a kelson of the creation is love' – Walt Whitman, *Leaves of Grass*.
Kilbride	'The cell or church of Bhrighde' – a common Scottish and Irish place-name, applied to the area and islands south of north Harris in pre-Reformation times.
Lacuna	An empty space or missing part, suggestive of loss (plural, *lacunae*).
Laird	Lord (Scots), especially a landlord.
Lazybeds	Raised beds (narrow strips of land) for growing crops, used especially where soil is thin and the ground waterlogged – in Gaelic, *feannagan*.
Lewisian Gneiss	The ancient metamorphic rock of the Isle of Lewis – 'gneiss' being an old German word for 'sparkling'.
Lithogenesis	The process of rock formation and thus, of the Earth itself.
Maieutic	The birthing art of a midwife, applied by Socrates to his way of teaching philosophy.
Metamorphic	Rocks, often very ancient, formed by re-crystallisation under intense heat and pressure.

Net of Indra	The Hindu-Buddhist idea that reality comprises a vast woven net, at each intersection of which is a jewel (or pearl) in which every other is reflected as mirrors to infinity. Thus the idea that every microcosm, or every person, contains the macrocosm, or all people.
Pearly Gates	A variety of the Morning Glory plant with psychedelic (i.e. 'mind-manifesting') properties.
Plutonic	Rocks such as granites and pegmatites, coarsely crystalline due to their formation from lenses of molten magma deep beneath the Earth's surface, cooled slowly. Named after Pluto, god of the underworld.
Prozac	An antidepressant drug that suppresses the appetite for reality.
Postmodernity	Modernity still professes to believe in itself, but postmodernity has lost that faith. Much of my own worldview is premodern or 'essentialist', believing that people and things can have an inner essence with intrinsic value that gives poetic meaning to the world.
Psyche	The totality of human being, body, mind, soul, and context of reality.
Roineabhal	The highest mountain in the National Scenic Area of south Harris, once threatened by a multinational corporation's superquarry proposal for roadstone. (Pron.: *Roin-è-val*.)

Saddhu	A wandering Indian holy man leading a life of simplicity.
Scythe	An elongated sickle, for cutting leaves of grass and, by metaphor, the lives of humankind.
Self	As used by Carl Jung, the soul or central constellating part of our psyche that is beyond ego.
Strimmer	A smelly, noisy, petrol-driven device with a rotating nylon string for cutting grass.
Tao	In Chinese philosophy, the equivalent of God transcendent, from which the manifest world of yin and yang forces pours forth and to which it returns.
Tectonics	The movement of continental plates of solid rock on the earth's surface over a semi-molten inner mantle, driven by convection currents of hot rock.
Tormentil	A little four-petalled yellow flower that grows in rich profusion in Scotland during the summer. My grandmother, on my father's side, taught me its name as 'tormetillo' at the side of our well when I was very young. It was the only meaningful connection I ever felt with her, which is perhaps why I associate it with the opening of the heart.

Transfiguration | A transformation that glorifies, exalts, and reveals inner essence.

Tree of Life | The tree whose fruit offered immortality, and which grew in Eden alongside the Tree of the Knowledge of Good and Evil. A symbol of realised spiritual life.

Usufruct | A diverse and often overlapping quilt-work of rights of land usage, in contrast to outright ownership and control. For example, one group might have traditional rights to fish from an area, while another will have the timber rights.

Waste Land, The | TS Eliot's influential poem about the loss of meaning in modernity.

Waulking | A rhythmic working of tweed cloth to soften it, undertaken by hand usually by a group of women, who might accompany their labour with 'waulking songs'. A form of 'wonted' work – work that is wanted, habitual and fitting to people and place, 'as is their wont'.

Let Me Dance with Your Shadow / Dannsam led Fhaileas

Martin MacIntyre / Martainn Mac an t-Saoir
ISBN 1 905222 57 2 PBK £8.99

Martin MacIntyre's first collection of poetry rejoices in the passion and vitality of human experience, showing a detailed observance of human emotion. He draws inspiration from the past whilst emphasising the continuity and contemporising of tradition, which confronts and often consoles his concerns over the inevitable passing of time. The reader is left with a sense of finding comfort and affirmation in the richness of everyday experience. A bilingual anthology in English and in Gaelic, *Let Me Dance with Your Shadow / Dannsam led Fhaileas* expressed universal themes of love, loss, and the joy of human experience, blending traditional Gaelic styles with a fresh, modern approach to writing.

Martin MacIntyre was winner of the 2003 Saltire Scottish First Book of the Year Award with *Ath – Aithne* and was shortlisted for the 2005 Saltire Scottish Book of the Year with *Gymnippers Diciadain*.

Accent o the Mind

Rab Wilson
ISBN 1 905222 32 7 PBK £8.99

The 'Mither o aa Pairlaments'? A sham! They've ne'er jaloused in mair's fowr hunner years, Whit maitters maist is whit's atween yer ears!

The joy, the pain, the fear, the anger and the shame – topical and contemporary, and mostly in vibrant Scots, this is Scottish poetry at its best. Encompassing history, text messaging, politics, asylum-seeking hedgehogs and Buckfast, Rab Wilson covers the variety of modern Scottish life through refreshingly honest and often humorous poetry. *Accent o the Mind* follows on from Rab Wilson's groundbreaking translation into Scots of the Persian epic, *The Ruba'iyat of Omar Khayyam*, with a Scots translation of Horace satires. It also includes sonnets inspired by the Miners' Strike of 1984-85; poems he scribed as a Wigtown Bard; and the results of being twinned with his local MSP.

This inspirational new collection consolidates Rab Wilson's position as one of Scotland's leading poets and plays a part in the reinvigoration of the Scots language in modern Scottish society.

Bursting with ambition, technically brilliant and funny

James W Wood, SCOTLAND ON SUNDAY

Lewis & Harris: History & Pre-History

Francis Thompson

ISBN 0 946487 77 4 PBK £4.99

The fierce Norsemen, intrepid missionaries and mighty Scottish clans - all have left a visible mark on the landscape of Lewis and Harris. This comprehensive guide explores sites of interest in the Western Isles, from pre-history through to the present day.

Harsh conditions failed to deter invaders from besieging these islands or intrepid travellers from settling, and their legacy has stood the test of time in an array of captivating archaeological remains from the stunningly preserved Carloway Broch, to a number of haunting standing stones, tombs and cairns. With captivating tales - including an intriguing murder mystery and a romantic encounter resulting in dramatic repercussions for warring clans - Francis Thompson introduces us to his homeland and gives us an insight into its forgotten ways of life.

Leaving behind a wondrous legacy of haunting standing stones and carved relics, such as the famous Lewis Chessmen. Captivating tales, passed down through generations, include an intriguing murder mystery and a romantic encounter resulting in dramatic repercussions for warring clans. Current places of archaeological interest are explored, as are celebrated sites such as the stunningly preserved Carloway Broch and evocative black houses, giving insights into a forgotten way of life.

Scotland – Land & People: An Inhabited Solitude

James McCarthy

ISBN 0 946487 57 X PBK £7.99

The new Scottish parliament is responsible for the environment of Scotland with the opportunity for land reform and new approaches to the protection and management of an incomparable countryside to meet the needs of the 21st century. It is difficult to avoid the conclusion that a far more radical approach is now required to safeguard the public interest over a very large proportion of Scotland's mountain and moorland country. There is little point in exhorting the unemployed, trapped in sub-standard inner city homes, to support campaigns for sustainable forestry or the protection of the Green Belt from industrial encroachment. The plain fact of the matter is that in Scotland, as elsewhere, the means of subsistence will always be first priority where this is under threat, and so-called environmentalists have too often been guilty of adopting an indifference to this.

Luath Press Limited

committed to publishing well written books worth reading

LUATH PRESS takes its name from Robert Burns, whose little collie Luath (*Gael.*, swift or nimble) tripped up Jean Armour at a wedding and gave him the chance to speak to the woman who was to be his wife and the abiding love of his life. Burns called one of *The Twa Dogs* Luath after Cuchullin's hunting dog in *Ossian's Fingal*. Luath Press was established in 1981 in the heart of Burns country, and is now based a few steps up the road from Burns' first lodgings on Edinburgh's Royal Mile.

Luath offers you distinctive writing with a hint of unexpected pleasures.

Most bookshops in the UK, the US, Canada, Australia, New Zealand and parts of Europe either carry our books in stock or can order them for you. To order direct from us, please send a £sterling cheque, postal order, international money order or your credit card details (number, address of cardholder and expiry date) to us at the address below. Please add post and packing as follows: UK – £1.00 per delivery address; overseas surface mail – £2.50 per delivery address; overseas airmail – £3.50 for the first book to each delivery address, plus £1.00 for each additional book by airmail to the same address. If your order is a gift, we will happily enclose your card or message at no extra charge.

Luath Press Limited
543/2 Castlehill
The Royal Mile
Edinburgh EH1 2ND
Scotland
Telephone: 0131 225 4326 (24 hours)
Fax: 0131 225 4324
email: sales@luath.co.uk
Website: www.luath.co.uk